Alpha Meditation

A nonreligious mindfulness exercise that produces synchronous Alpha frequency brainwaves

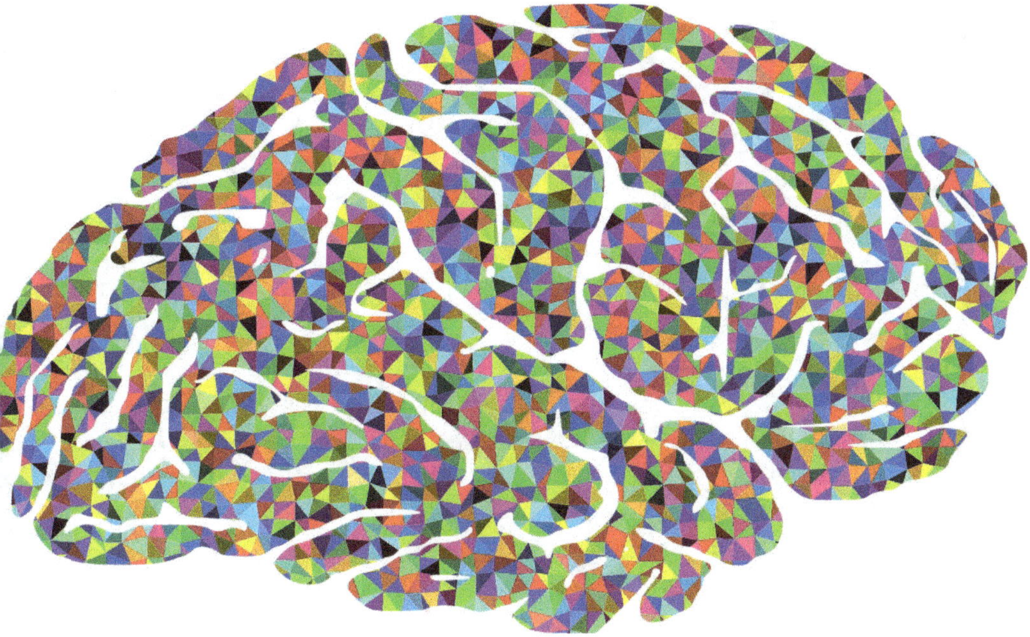

BY
Regi Belton

Copyright 2019 All rights reserved
Puppet Theater Books
Dewey location: 158.12

Have you ever been

scared?

Or nervous?

Or angry?

Can your mind be **noisy**?

If you've ever been

scared

or nervous

or angry

then this exercise will help you control your mind, and quite the

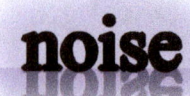
noise

Your mind is
AMAZING.

Your mind
can think
fast and slow,
in different parts,
at the
same time.

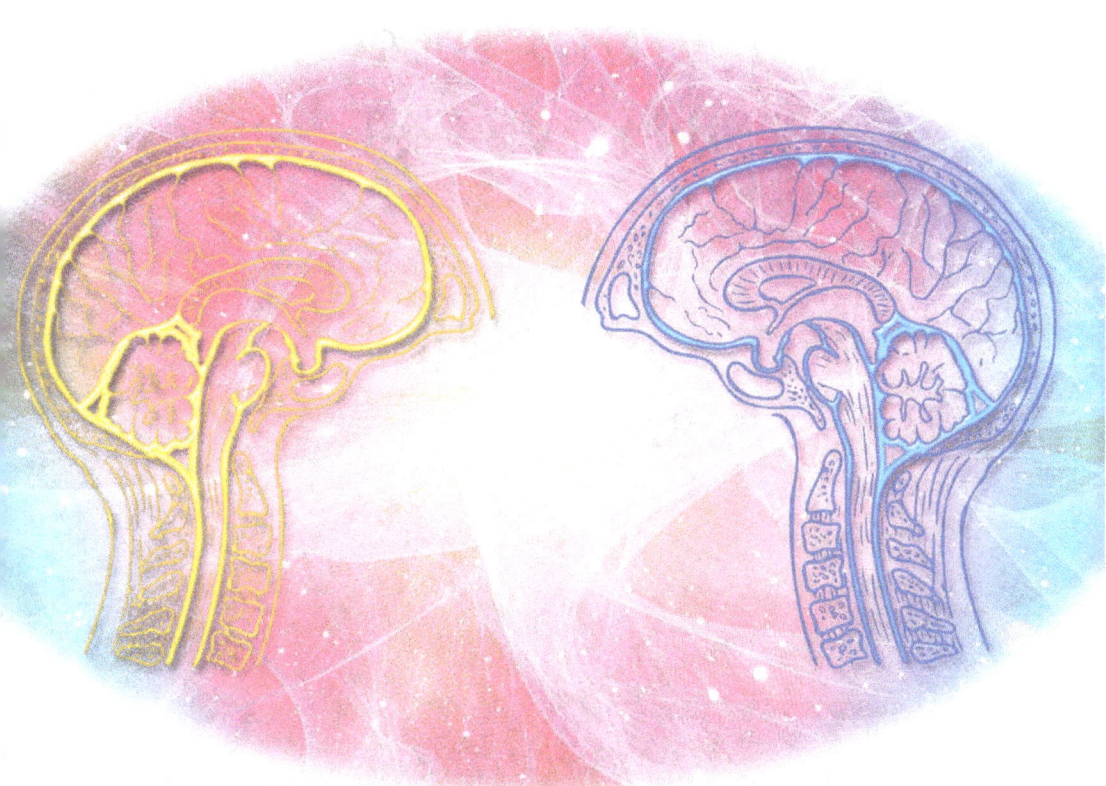

This can be

noisy

making us feel unsettled,
but if we get all the parts
working together at the same
Alpha speed,
then we feel
peaceful,
focused,
and quiet.

Find a quiet,
comfortable
place,
and close your eyes.

Perfect.

Now, simply *relax* your feet.
Let all the **tension** out.
Good.

Now *relax* your legs,
then your hips.
Feel them *soften* and *relax*.
Good.

Relax your chest and arms.
Now your shoulders.

And finally,
relax your neck and head.
Good. That feels **good**.

Notice your breath,
the air flowing
in and out
of your mouth or nose.

Notice the air going
in and out,
in and out.

Good.

Notice your belly
going up and down
with your breath,
going up and down
with the air
going in and out,
up and down,
in and out.

Good.

Notice that.

Good.

Let's move to your eyes now.
Notice the space
between your eyes.

Good.

Can you place yourself there?

Keep your eyes closed
and imagine
the space between your eyes,
as you breathe in and out,
in and out.

Good.

Good....

Now, notice the space
between your ears.

Place yourself there,
in the space
between your ears,
as you breathe in and out,
breathe in and out.

Your mind will want to go
other places,
to think about
other things.

Every time it does that,
simply place yourself
back between your ears,
as you breathe
in
and
out.

Stay between your ears.

Stay there.

Good.

Stay there.

Good....

This is your **Alpha** place.

Feel how calm you are?

See how your mind is quiet?

You are safe and at peace.

Stay for a while,
here between your ears.
Stay in your **Alpha** place,
as long as you like.

Just stay,
and enjoy.

When you are ready to leave
your **Alpha** place,
notice your belly,
going up and down,
your breath,
going in and out,
and slowly,
slowly,
open your eyes….

Wherever you go, whatever you feel, your **Alpha** place is with you.

To control your mind and quiet the noise, simply close your eyes, breathe in and out, and place yourself between your ears.

You may stay
in your
Alpha place
until you feel

ready

and

safe

to join the world around you.